E
VEGETARIAN
RECIPES

compiled by
Marilyn Membery

Illustrated with
cottage garden
scenes

SALMON

Index

Artichoke, Walnut and
  Goat's Cheese Paté 27
Aubergine Bake 5
Broad Bean Cannelloni 4
Butter Bean Hotpot 7
Carrot and Red Lentil Soup 8
Cheese and Broccoli Pasta Puff 10
Cheese, Onion and Herb Plait 11
Cheese and Walnut Roast 14
Cheese Pudding 15
Cheesy Biscuits 16
Cheesy Sliced Potatoes 13
Chestnut and Red Wine Pie 18
Courgette Bake 19
Chick Pea Stew 21
Glamorgan Sausages 22
Goat's Cheese Risotto 23
Fruit and Nut Rice Salad 24

Lentil and Tomato Quiche 26
Marrow, Onion and Tomato Gratin 29
Mushroom, Lentil and
  Cheese Wedge 30
Mushrooms Stuffed with Stilton 31
Nut Roast 32
Onion and Goat's Cheese Tarts 34
Pumpkin Soup 35
Quorn Fillets in Thyme Sauce 37
Roasted Goat's Cheese Tart 39
Roasted Tomato Sauce 38
Sausages with Caramelised Onions 40
Savoury Crumble 42
Spinach Bread and Butter Bake 43
Stuffed Aubergines 45
Swedish Potatoes 46
Vegetable Lasagne, Roast vegetables
  Lasagne 47

Cover pictures *front:* "At the Cottage Door" *by Myles Birkett Foster*
back: "An Afternoon in the Garden" *by Myles Birkett Foster*
Title page: "The Cabbage Patch" *by Alfred Glendening*
Facing page: "A Cottage Garden" *by Walter Langley*

Printed and Published by J. Salmon Ltd., Sevenoaks, England © Copyright

Broad Bean Cannelloni

*The first time I made this one of my guests didn't like broad beans but decided to try it.
I had to give her the recipe afterwards.*

12 cannelloni tubes	¾ pint white sauce
8 oz. broad beans, fresh or frozen	1 tub of soft cheese
1 clove of garlic, crushed	Chopped fresh chives (handful)
1 quantity of tomato sauce (see page 38)	Nutmeg, grated

4 tablespoons grated Parmesan

Cook the broad beans, drain and refresh with cold water. Put beans, cheese, garlic, chives and nutmeg in a food processor, season with black pepper and pulse until it is all combined but not too smooth. Put the tomato sauce in the bottom of an oven-proof dish. Fill the cannelloni with the broad bean mixture and place over the tomato. Cover with the white sauce, sprinkle with parmesan and bake at 350°F or Mark 4 for 40 minutes.

Aubergine Bake

Aubergines are delicious when cooked like this. All the individual flavours marry together but still come through when eating it.

4 aubergines   **1 whole bulb of garlic**
2 tins cherry tomatoes   **1 large ball of mozzarella**
Grated Parmesan

Slice the aubergines long ways into thick slices. Griddle or fry the slices on each side for about two minutes. Put on one side to cool. Heat the tomatoes in a pan for a few minutes. Put a slice of aubergine in the bottom of an oven-proof dish. Top with tomatoes, sliced garlic cloves, and slices of mozzarella. Continue to layer the bake until all is used. Cover with foil and bake at 350°F or Mark 4 for 40 minutes. Remove the foil for the last ten minutes. Grate the parmesan over the top and finish in the oven. Serves 2.

Butter Bean Hotpot

This is a simple recipe but it makes a delicious main course.

1 tin of butter beans	1 tablespoon plain flour
3 oz. broad beans (frozen)	4 oz. soft cheese
6 oz. carrots sliced thinly	6 oz. parsnips sliced thinly
1 tub cream cheese	6 oz. swede cut into cubes
1 tablespoon olive oil or butter	1¼ pints of vegetable stock

Any fresh herbs – thyme, parsley, tarragon or any you have
Black pepper to taste

Cook the vegetables (except the beans) in the vegetable stock. Just before the vegetables are cooked add the beans and heat them through. Drain the vegetables and keep them warm but keep half a pint of the stock. Heat olive oil (or melt butter if preferred), sprinkle over the flour and then gradually add the stock stirring all the time. Once you have a smooth sauce leave it to simmer gently. Whisk in the cream cheese and season with black pepper. Pour over the hot vegetables and serve with brown rice. Serves 4.

Carrot and Red Lentil Soup

This soup is a real favourite for church meals.

6 oz. onions peeled and sliced   **4 oz. dried red lentils washed**
12 oz. carrots peeled and sliced   **1½ pints stock (made with a stock cube is fine)**
2 teaspoons of oil

Heat the oil, and add the onions and carrots. Once softened, but not browned, add the lentils and stir well. Add the stock, stirring well. Put a lid on the pan and bring to the boil. Turn down the heat to simmer. Cook for about 45 minutes – the lentils should be soft and the soup fairly thick. Cool the mixture and then blend, adding more stock if necessary.

"Near Hambledon" by Helen Allingha

Cheese and Broccoli Pasta Puff

No child (or adult) will refuse to eat broccoli served like this!

1¾ oz. butter plus extra for greasing   1 pint of milk
8 oz. mini pasta shapes   3 oz. extra strong cheese
6 oz. small broccoli florets   1 tablespoon of wholegrain mustard
1¾ oz. plain flour   3 eggs, separated

Salt and pepper

Grease a two pint ovenproof dish. Cook the pasta and broccoli until tender.
Melt the butter and stir in the flour. Add the milk and bring to the boil stirring
constantly. Once thickened, stir in the mustard, add salt and pepper and
simmer gently for 2 to 3 minutes. Stir in the cheese and put on one side to cool.
Add the pasta, broccoli and egg yolks, stirring well. Whisk the egg whites until
stiff, then fold into the pasta. Spoon the mixture into the dish and bake at
400°F or Mark 6 for 20 minutes.

Cheese, Onion and Herb Plait

This can also be served with soup instead of bread.

8 oz. self-raising flour	**1 egg**
3 oz. margarine	**¼ pint of milk**
4 oz. mature Cheddar cheese grated	**2 teaspoons of mixed herbs**
½ onion chopped finely	**Black pepper**

Sift the flour with the herbs and black pepper. Rub the fat into the flour and add the cheese and onion. Beat the egg and milk together. Add the liquid a little at a time until it forms a soft dough. Turn the dough onto a floured board and divide into three. Roll each piece into a long sausage shape, then plait the pieces together. Brush with the left-over egg and bake at 425°F or Mark 7 for 10-15 minutes. This is best eaten on the day you make it.

Cheesy Sliced Potatoes

This is my "comfort food" dish. I always have it with home-made sausages.

2 large potatoes, scrubbed well or peeled and sliced
1 large onion sliced thinly   4 oz. mature cheese, grated
2 eggs beaten   ½ pint of milk
1 casserole, greased lightly

Put the potatoes in the dish and layer up with onions and cheese, finishing with the cheese. Beat the eggs and stir in the milk. Strain the liquid into the casserole and bake for one hour at 350°F or Mark 4. Serves 2.

Cheese and Walnut Roast

Unusual, but certainly worth trying.

6 oz. walnuts	**2 tablespoons of fresh parsley chopped**
6 oz. wholemeal breadcrumbs	**5 tablespoons of hot milk**
3 oz. Cheddar cheese grated	**½ oz. butter**
1 onion grated	**1 teaspoon of English mustard**

Grind the nuts and add the rest of the ingredients (except the butter and milk) to the processor. Tip into a bowl and stir in the milk. Shape into a round. Grease a piece of foil and place the roast on top. Dot on the butter, wrap up the foil and bake at 350°F or Mark 4 for 40 minutes. Serve with home-made tomato sauce and vegetables. Serves 4.

Cheese Pudding

This is a really simple recipe, but served with salad it is quick, easy and tasty.

4 oz. bread   1 oz butter   2 eggs   ½ pint of milk
6 oz. grated cheese (reserve 1 oz. for later)
Black pepper   Greased oven-proof dish
I always eat brown bread but for this recipe I like to use white bread

Dice the bread and put in the dish. Warm the milk and add the butter. Beat the eggs and add the milk, cheese and pepper. Stir well and pour over the bread. I always leave this dish for at least an hour before baking. When you take it out of the oven it is all golden and puffy. Bake for 30 minutes at 375°F or Mark 5. Serve immediately. Serves 2.

Cheesy Biscuits

I like to use these when serving cheese; it is good to have home-made biscuits.

4 oz. wholewheat flour	**A pinch of cayenne pepper**
½ teaspoon salt	**4 oz. mature Cheddar cheese, grated**
¼ teaspoon black pepper	**4 oz. Parmesan cheese, grated**
	4 oz. butter

Sieve the flour, salt and pepper into a bowl. Add both the cheeses and rub the butter into the flour, gradually bringing the mixture together. Wrap in cling film and pop in the fridge for a few minutes. Roll out to the thickness of a £1 coin, cut with a biscuit cutter and bake on greased trays at 375°F or Mark 5 for 10-15 minutes.

"A Country Cottage" by Helen Allingham

Chestnut and Red Wine Pie

This makes an attractive centrepiece for Christmas Day.

12 oz. can of unsweetened chestnut purée   1 oz. butter
2 medium onions, sliced   2 garlic cloves, crushed
2 oz. mushrooms, chopped   1 leek, finely chopped
3 fluid oz. of red wine   3 oz. white breadcrumbs
2 tablespoons of cranberry sauce
1 lb. flaky pastry   1 egg beaten for glazing

Melt the butter in a pan and fry the onions, garlic and leeks. Add the mushrooms and continue to cook. Pour in the red wine and let it bubble away. Once it is slightly thickened, remove and stir in the breadcrumbs and chestnut purée. Roll out the pastry into two strips, one longer than the other. Put the smaller one on a greased baking tray and spoon the mixture on and carefully spread the cranberry sauce over the top. Brush the edges all the way round with cold water. Carefully put the larger piece of pastry over the top and seal well. Cut the leftover pastry into Christmas shapes to decorate the pie. Glaze with the beaten egg. Bake at 400°F or Mark 6 for 50 minutes.

Courgette Bake

Delicious and good with a green salad for lunch time.

4 medium courgettes, washed and grated
1 onion, chopped finely
4 oz. extra strong Cheddar cheese
4 slices of vegetarian bacon grilled until brown and chopped into pieces
1 oz. butter, melted   Black pepper   3 eggs
2 large tomatoes, sliced

Put the eggs in a large bowl and beat well. Add the other ingredients except the tomatoes. Pour into a greased oven-proof dish, top with tomatoes and bake at 350°F or Mark 4 for 35-40 minutes. Serves 2.

Chick Pea Stew

This stew is delicious served with mashed potatoes and vegetables.

1 tin of chick peas	1 red pepper, sliced
2 tins of chopped tomatoes	1 yellow pepper, sliced
2 onions, chopped	2 aubergines, chopped
1 garlic clove, crushed	Fresh coriander to taste

1 teaspoon of oil

Heat the oil and fry the onion and garlic together. Add the aubergine and then add all the rest of the ingredients. Stir well, put in an oven-proof dish and cook in the oven at 375°F or Mark 5 for 45-60 minutes.

Glamorgan Sausages

*I have tried lots of home-made sausages; a friend gave me this recipe
and I cannot find a better one.*

4 oz. wholemeal breadcrumbs   **1 teaspoon dried marjoram**
6 oz. Caerphilly cheese, crumbled **1 tablespoon coarse grain mustard**
2 tablespoons finely chopped leeks   **Black pepper**
2 eggs (1 separated)

Coating:
2 oz. breadcrumbs (white bread if you have it, otherwise wholemeal)
1 egg white

Mix the breadcrumbs, cheese, leeks, mustard, herbs and pepper together. Bind the mixture with the whole egg and the extra egg yolk. Make into sausage shapes. Dip the sausages in the egg white and then the breadcrumbs. Put them in the fridge for about an hour before shallow frying them.

Goat's Cheese Risotto

*It took me a long while to attempt risotto but this is so simple
I enjoy making it and my family enjoy eating it!*

11 oz. risotto rice	**1 litre of vegetable stock**
1 onion, finely chopped	**1 packet of goat's cheese**
1 clove of garlic, crushed	**Asparagus**
½ oz. butter	

Fry the onions in the melted butter. Add the garlic and once softened add the rice, stirring well. Add a quarter of the stock and stir well. Once the stock is absorbed continue adding the stock until it is all used. Once the risotto is cooked take off the heat and add pieces of goat's cheese. Stir well and keep warm. Griddle the asparagus for two or three minutes. Serve the risotto topped with the asparagus. Serves 2.

Fruit and Nut Rice Salad

*If we are having a meal at church this is something I like to take
served on a pretty dish; it makes a good centrepiece.*

3 oz. sultanas or large raisins	½ red pepper, deseeded and chopped
6 oz. dried fruit – apples, apricots	2 oz. butter
1 tablespoon sweet sherry	1 onion, finely chopped
1 oz. almonds	Black pepper
1 oz. pine nuts	½ teaspoon of all spice

8 oz. rice, cooked (white or brown)

Put the dried fruit in a bowl and sprinkle with the sherry. Add two tablespoons of cold water, stir well and leave to soak, stirring occasionally. When plump drain the liquid off and chop finely. Grease an oven-proof dish. Put the rest of the butter in a frying pan and fry the onion until softened. Add the rice and all the other ingredients. Put in the oven and heat through for 15 minutes at 375°F or Mark 5. This is delicious warm, but also makes a good pack-up for the next day.

"Springtime" by Helen Allingham

Lentil and Tomato Quiche

*This is a good wholesome quiche, it can also be covered
with a pastry top and made into a pie.*

1 lb. of shortcrust pastry	1 clove of garlic, crushed
2 oz. mature Cheddar cheese	6 oz. green lentils (tinned or cooked)
1 tablespoon of oil	1 tin chopped tomatoes
2 onions, chopped	8 fluid oz. water
2 celery sticks, chopped	1 tablespoon fresh parsley, chopped

Roll out the pastry, line a flan dish and bake blind for 10-15 minutes at 400°F
or Mark 6. Heat the oil and fry the onions, celery and garlic until soft. Add
the tomatoes, lentils and water. Cover and simmer for 1 hour. When the
mixture is thick stir in the parsley and put into the prepared flan case. Sprinkle
the grated cheese over the top and bake for 15-20 minutes at 400°F or Mark 6.
Serves 4.

Artichoke, Walnut and Goat's Cheese Paté

I always serve roasted peppers with this paté.

1 tin artichoke hearts   4 oz. goat's cheese
2 oz. walnuts finely chopped
3 peppers (red or yellow or a mixture of both)
2 tablespoons of oil
4 tablespoons of balsamic vinegar

Chop the artichokes until small. Mash the goat's cheese and add the artichokes and walnuts. Mix well. Put in a dish, cover and leave in the fridge until ready to serve.

Place the halved peppers under a hot grill until the skin is blackened. Put them in a polythene bag and once cooled, peel and slice into thick slices into a dish. Mix the oil and vinegar together, pour over the pepper and leave to marinate.

Marrow, Onion and Tomato Gratin

This recipe is one my mother used to cook.

1 medium marrow	1 tablespoon of oil
2 large onions, chopped	2 teaspoons of mixed dried herbs
2 cloves of garlic, crushed	2 oz. mature cheese
1 large tin of tomatoes	2 oz. wholemeal breadcrumbs

Peel and deseed the marrow and cut into medium chunks. Heat the oil and cook the onions and garlic until softened. Add the tomatoes and marrow. Add the herbs, bring to the boil, cover and simmer. Once the marrow is cooked pour into an oven-proof dish. Mix the cheese and breadcrumbs together and sprinkle over the marrow. Put under a pre-heated grill until the breadcrumbs are golden. Serves 4.

Mushroom, Lentil and Cheese Wedge

Wonderful served hot, but leftovers make a tasty snack.

8 oz. red lentils
¾ pint of water
2 oz. mushrooms, wiped and chopped
1 large onion, peeled and chopped
1 oz. wholemeal breadcrumbs

1 oz. butter
4 oz. mature cheese, grated
1 teaspoon of dried parsley
½ teaspoon of mixed herbs
1 egg, beaten

Cook the lentils in the water until soft and all the liquid has evaporated. Melt the butter in a saucepan and fry the onions. Add the mushrooms and continue to cook. Once cooked, combine all the ingredients together and press into a greased sandwich tin. Bake in the oven at 375°F or Mark 5 for 20 minutes. I sometimes put sliced tomatoes on the top before baking. Serves 4.

Mushrooms Stuffed with Stilton

I use these as a starter when I have guests, but at home we eat them as a main course. Either way they are delicious.

4 large mushrooms	**2 cloves of garlic, crushed**
1 oz. butter	**4 oz. Stilton, crumbled**
1 onion, chopped finely	**2 oz. wholemeal breadcrumbs**
2 tablespoons red wine	**Black pepper**

Wipe the mushrooms, remove the stalks and reserve them. Grease an oven-proof tray and cook the mushrooms for five minutes. Chop the mushroom stalks. Heat the butter in a pan and cook the onions and garlic. Add the mushroom stalks and once softened add the wine and turn up the heat. Cook for a couple of minutes. Take off the heat and stir in the breadcrumbs and stilton cheese and black pepper. Cover the mushrooms with the mixture and bake in the oven at 400°F or Mark 6 for 10-15 minutes.

Nut Roast

This is the best nut roast I know of.

6 oz. brown rice, cooked	4 oz. fresh wholemeal breadcrumbs
½ oz. butter	4 oz. mixed nuts, chopped finely
1 medium onion, chopped finely	4 oz. mature cheese, grated
1 clove of crushed garlic	2 eggs, beaten well
2 carrots, grated	Black pepper
4 oz. mushrooms, chopped finely	2 lb. loaf tin, lined

Melt the butter and cook the onion, garlic, carrot and mushrooms. Stir in the breadcrumbs, nuts, rice, cheese and eggs. Season with pepper and mix well. Put in the loaf tin and bake at 350°F or Mark 4 for 1-1¼ hours.

"Cottage Garden at Sandhills" by Helen Allingham

Onion and Goat's Cheese Tarts

I was afraid of using filo pastry, but once you try it you see how easy it is.

8 oz. pack of filo pastry	4 tablespoons balsamic vinegar
8 oz. goat's cheese	1 tablespoon brown sugar
2 oz. butter, melted	1 teaspoon dried thyme
1 lb. red onions	1 packet of rocket leaves

Cut 18 pieces of filo pastry about 6 inch square, and use to line six small bun tins. Brush each piece with a little melted butter and chill in the fridge.

Peel and slice the onions into thick slices. Fry in the oil for ten to fifteen minutes. When the onions are soft add the balsamic vinegar and sprinkle the brown sugar over. Continue to cook until almost all the liquid has evaporated and the onions have a glaze to them. Bake the tarts in the oven at 350°F or Mark 4 until golden in colour and crisp. Remove from the oven and turn the oven down to 300°F or Mark 2. Stir the rocket through the onions until it wilts, then spoon into the cases. Sprinkle a little thyme onto each tartlet and then drizzle the goat's cheese over the top and bake for about ten minutes until the cheese has melted.

Pumpkin Soup

This is a delicious, creamy soup.

**1 lb. pumpkin peeled, seeded and chopped
1 medium onion, peeled and chopped
1 medium potato, peeled and chopped   1 oz. butter
3 cups of vegetable stock   1 teaspoon of brown sugar
½ teaspoon of paprika   Salt and pepper
Grated nutmeg to taste**

Melt the butter and fry the onions, but do not allow them to brown. Add the potato and pumpkin and sprinkle over the sugar, mixing well. Pour in the stock and bring to the boil. Put the lid on the pan, then turn down the heat and allow to simmer for thirty minutes. Add the spice and grated nutmeg. Put in a liquidiser and serve.

Quorn Fillets in Thyme Sauce

A delicious and creamy recipe.

4 Quorn fillets   **Thyme chopped finely**
½ oz. butter   **1 oz. butter**
1 onion, finely chopped (optional)   **1 oz. plain flour**
2 oz. mushrooms, sliced (optional)   **½ pint of milk**
¼ pint of water

Melt the butter and add the onions and mushrooms. Brown the fillets and put in an oven-proof dish. Wipe the frying pan, then melt 1 oz of butter. Sprinkle over the flour. Add the milk and water slowly and stir all the time until you have a smooth sauce. Stir in the thyme. Pour over the fillets and put in the oven for 20-25 minutes at 350°F or Mark 4. Serve with potatoes or vegetables, but another favourite way is to serve it on a bed of brown rice.

Roasted Tomato Sauce

This is delicious served with pasta.   An excellent sauce to have in your freezer.

2 lb. red tomatoes   **2 tablespoons of olive oil**
½ bunch of basil   **2 tablespoons of balsamic vinegar**
2 cloves of garlic, sliced   **Salt and pepper**

Cut the tomatoes in half and put on a baking tray, cut side up. Season with salt and pepper. Sprinkle 1 tablespoon of oil over them. Dip the basil leaves in the other tablespoon of oil. Put a slice of garlic and a basil leaf on each tomato. Roast the tomatoes in the oven until the edges are blackened. Scrape all the tomatoes and the juices into a food processor. Add the vinegar and whiz together. Gently reheat the sauce.

Roasted Goat's Cheese Tart

This looks really impressive and can be used as a starter for a dinner party.
I have made individual ones.

1 lb. tomatoes	**5 oz. goat's cheese**
2 teaspoons of dried thyme	**2 cloves of garlic, crushed**
¾ lb. flaky pastry	**Black pepper**
1-2 teaspoons of oil	**Greased baking tray**
	Fresh basil leaves

Roll the pastry into a square and put on the baking tray. Using a sharp knife, score a line all the way round about ½ an inch from the edge of the pastry, but do not cut all the way through. Put into a bowl the goat's cheese, thyme, pepper and garlic and mix together. Spread over the pastry using a flat-bladed knife. Thinly slice the tomatoes and arrange over the cheese. Season with salt and pepper. Drizzle the olive oil over the tomatoes, sprinkle with torn basil leaves and bake at 350°F or Mark 4 for 35 minutes. Serves 4.

Sausages with Caramelised Onions

This is delicious and one of my favourite recipes.

2 teaspoons of oil	**2 teaspoons balsamic vinegar**
2 oz. goat's cheese	**1 packet of vegetarian sausages**
1 teaspoon of demerara sugar	**1 medium red onion, sliced finely**

Heat the oil and fry the onions. Add the vinegar and boil for a minute until the liquid is like syrup. Sprinkle over the sugar and simmer gently with the mixture to become caramelised and sticky. Cook the sausages separately, then put in an oven-proof dish. Pour the onion mixture over the top and dot with goat's cheese. Put under the hot grill until the goat's cheese is melted.

"A Surrey Cottage" by Helen Allingha

Savoury Crumble

A brilliant way to introduce children to brussel sprouts!

1 lb. potatoes, peeled and cut into 4   8 oz. leeks, sliced
1 lb. carrots, chopped   12 oz. brussel sprouts, sliced thinly
4 oz. mushrooms, sliced   1 oz. butter

Crumble
2 oz. plain flour   1 oz. oats   2 oz. butter   2 oz. mature cheese
2 tablespoons parsley, chopped   ½ teaspoon mustard powder

Add the potatoes to a pan of water, bring to the boil and cook for fifteen minutes. Melt the butter in a large pan. Add the leeks and carrots and cook over a low heat for two or three minutes. Add the mushrooms and cook for a further two or three minutes. Add the sliced brussels to the pan. Transfer the vegetables to a deep oven-proof dish. Once the potatoes have cooled sufficiently to handle, cut into half-inch slices and top the vegetables with these. Make the crumble by rubbing the butter into the flour and mustard powder until it is like breadcrumbs. Add the other ingredients and mix well. Sprinkle over the vegetables and bake at 375°F or Mark 5 for about 20 minutes. Serves 4.

Spinach Bread and Butter Bake

This is a really delicious savoury bread pudding. My vegetarian friends all ask me to make it when they are coming for a meal.

1 bag of spinach	4 oz. Gruyere cheese, grated
Ciabatta loaf, sliced	3 eggs
1 red onion, sliced	¾ pint milk
4 oz. mushrooms, sliced	1 teaspoon of mixed herbs
Grated nutmeg	

Blanch the washed spinach, drain well and chop finely. Put the bread slices in an oven-proof greased dish. Fry the onions and the mushrooms. Add the spinach and the herbs and season well. Layer the bread and spinach mixture and half the cheese, finishing with bread. Beat the eggs and milk together and pour over the bread. Sprinkle the remaining cheese over the top. Sprinkle with nutmeg and leave for at least an hour before baking at 375°F or Mark 5 for 45 minutes.

Stuffed Aubergines

Serve these with a green salad. They are really delicious and very filling.

2 aubergines	2 oz. mushrooms, sliced
1 tablespoon of oil	6 tablespoons brown rice, cooked
1 onion, chopped	1 oz. pine nuts, roasted
2 sticks of celery, chopped	1 tablespoon of tomato purée
2 oz. cheese, grated	Salt and pepper
1 tin of tomatoes	1 clove of garlic, crushed

1 tablespoon of dried parsley

Cut the aubergines in half, put on a greased baking tray and cook for about 15 minutes. Fry the onion and garlic together. Add the celery and mushrooms, cooking until tender, and then add the rice, tinned tomatoes, tomato purée and parsley. Once the aubergines are cool, take out the flesh, chop and add to the mixture. Spoon it back into the skins and sprinkle the grated cheese over the top. Put under the grill until the cheese has melted.

Swedish Potatoes

I make this for Sunday lunch. Sometimes its amazing how many meat eaters become vegetarian when this is the meal of the day!

1 swede, sliced very thinly
1 baking potato, sliced very thinly
2 sweet potatoes, sliced very thinly
3 garlic cloves, sliced very thinly
1 large onion, sliced thinly

A couple of pinches of paprika
2 oz. wild mushrooms
5 oz. double cream
2 teaspoons of olive oil

Layer the swede and potatoes in a dish. Drizzle the olive oil over the vegetables and bake for 25 minutes at 350°F or Mark 4. Fry the onions, garlic and mushrooms together, stir in the cream and pour over the potatoes. Sprinkle the paprika over the top and cook for a further 10 minutes. Serves 4.

Vegetable Lasagne

This takes a while to prepare but is well worth it.

1 aubergine, chopped
1 red and yellow pepper, chopped
1 quantity of tomato sauce (see page 38)
½ pint of white sauce
Olive oil

½ bunch of basil
2 red onions, peeled and quartered
2 courgettes, chopped
9 sheets of pasta
Freshly grated Parmesan

Put two tablespoons of oil in a large bowl and add the chopped vegetables, mixing them round to coat them. Put on a baking tray and put them in the oven to roast until just cooked. Mix the vegetables in the tomato sauce, season with black pepper and stir in the torn basil leaves. Lightly oil the lasagne dish. Put half the white sauce on the base, then layer the lasagne and tomato filling, ending with the pasta sheets. Cover with white sauce and bake at 375°F or Mark 5 for 35-40 minutes. Once baked, grate Parmesan cheese over the top and serve. Serves 4.

METRIC CONVERSIONS

The weights, measures and oven temperatures used in the preceding recipes can be easily converted to their metric equivalents. The conversions listed below are only approximate, having been rounded up or down as may be appropriate.

Weights

Avoirdupois	Metric
1 oz.	just under 30 grams
4 oz. (¼ lb.)	app. 115 grams
8 oz. (½ lb.)	app. 230 grams
1 lb.	454 grams

Liquid Measures

Imperial	Metric
1 tablespoon (liquid only)	20 millilitres
1 fl. oz.	app. 30 millilitres
1 gill (¼ pt.)	app. 145 millilitres
½ pt.	app. 285 millilitres
1 pt.	app. 570 millilitres
1 qt.	app. 1.140 litres

Oven Temperatures

	°Fahrenheit	Gas Mark	°Celsius
Slow	300	2	150
	325	3	170
Moderate	350	4	180
	375	5	190
	400	6	200
Hot	425	7	220
	450	8	230
	475	9	240

Flour as specified in these recipes refers to plain flour unless otherwise described.

Please note, where cheese is specified in these recipes either ordinary cheese or vegetarian cheese may be used.